T0096511

SPIRIT
of
FAITH

SPIRIT

of

FAITH

SACRIFICE
and
SERVICE

compiled by Bahá'í Publishing

Bahá'í
PUBLISHING

Wilmette, Illinois

Bahá'í Publishing
415 Linden Avenue, Wilmette, Illinois 60091-2844
Copyright © 2013 by the National Spiritual Assembly
of the Bahá'ís of the United States

All rights reserved. Published 2013
Printed in the United States of America on acid-free
paper ∞

16   15   14   13   4   3   2   1

Library of Congress Cataloging-in-Publication Data

Sacrifice and service / compiled by Baha'i Publishing.
     pages cm. — (Spirit of faith)
  Includes bibliographical references.
  ISBN 978-1-61851-031-0 (alk. paper)
 1. Bahai Faith—Doctrines. 2. Sacrifice—Bahai Faith.
3. Service (Theology) I. Bahá'u'lláh, 1817–1892.
Selections. 2013. II. Bab, 'Ali Muhammad Shirazi,
1819–1850. Selections. 2013. III. 'Abdu'l-Bahá,
1844–1921. Selections. 2013. IV. Baha'i Publishing.
 BP360.S23 2013
 297.9'32—dc23

                                        2012048282

Cover design by Andrew Johnson
Book design by Patrick Falso

CONTENTS

INTRODUCTION

Sacrifice and Service is the sixth book in Bahá'í Publishing's *Spirit of Faith* series, which continues to explore weighty spiritual topics—including the unity of the world's religions, the experience of the human soul after death, and the promise of world peace—by taking an in-depth look at how the writings of the Bahá'í Faith address these issues. It is hoped that meditation on the passages presented here will lead to profound and rewarding conversations.

The Bahá'í Faith is an independent world religion that began in 1844 in Persia (present-day Iran). Since its inception, the Bahá'í Faith has spread to

235 nations and territories and has been accepted by more than five million people. Bahá'ís believe that there is only one God, that all the major world religions come from God, and that all the members of the human race are essentially members of one family. Bahá'ís strive to eliminate all forms of prejudice and believe that people of all races, nations, social status, and religious backgrounds are equal in the sight of God. The Bahá'í Faith also teaches that each individual is responsible for the independent investigation of truth, that science and religion are in harmony, and that men and women are equal in the sight of God.

This volume is made up of passages related to the themes of sacrifice and service. Bahá'ís believe that one way that we can serve God is through service to humanity. Often, service in this form entails giving up personal desires but in some circumstances can even mean giving up one's life. Bahá'u'lláh, the

Founder of the Bahá'í Faith, specifically instructs His followers to expend all that they have for the unification and betterment of humanity and promises that great blessings are guaranteed to those who suffer hardship in the cause of the betterment of the world. 'Abdu'l-Bahá continues to elucidate the benefits of sacrifice by using the past Messengers of God as examples of the importance of this supreme act, and offers examples within the natural world to illustrate the principle. Many of these examples illustrate that sacrifice is not merely loss of something but is instead an exchange for something far better, though we may not always perceive or comprehend the benefits.

Included in this book are the writings of Bahá'u'lláh, the Founder of the Bahá'í Faith, considered by Bahá'ís to be the supreme Manifestation of God for the age in which we live; the writings of His forerunner, the Báb; and the writings and recorded utterances of Bahá'u'lláh's son and appointed successor, 'Abdu'l-Bahá. It is hoped that readers of all faiths and backgrounds will find the passages collected here to be thought-provoking and inspiring, and that meditation on these subjects will lead to new insights and understandings.

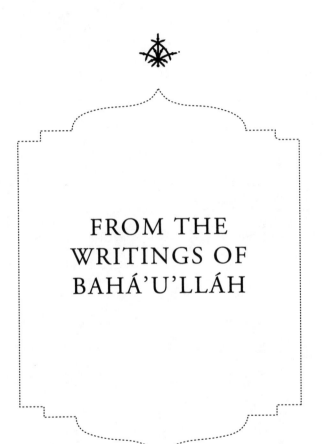

FROM THE
WRITINGS OF
BAHÁ'U'LLÁH

1

By the righteousness of God! If thou wert present before My Throne and didst hearken unto the Tongue of might and grandeur, thou wouldst sacrifice thy body, thy soul, thine entire being as a token of thy love for God, the Sovereign, the Protector, the All-Knowing, the All-Wise, and wouldst so thrill to the fascination of His Voice that every pen would be powerless to recount thy station and every eloquent speaker would be confounded in his attempt to describe it. Ponder a while concerning this Revelation and its invincible sovereignty; aid it then as it beseemeth thy Lord, the Gracious, the All-Bountiful.

2

Happy is the man who will arise to serve My Cause, and glorify My beauteous Name. Take hold of My Book with the power of My might, and cleave tenaciously to whatsoever commandment thy Lord, the Ordainer, the All-Wise, hath prescribed therein.

3

Blessed is he who hath heard of My grief and hath arisen to aid Me among My people. Blessed is he who hath laid down his life in My path and hath borne manifold hardships for the sake of My Name.

4

Thou art He, O God, Who hath proclaimed Himself as the Lord of Wealth, and characterized all that serve Him as poor and needy. Even as Thou hast written: "O ye that believe! Ye are but paupers in need of God; but God is the All-Possessing, the All-Praised." Having acknowledged my poverty, and recognized Thy wealth, suffer me not to be deprived of the glory of Thy riches. Thou art, verily, the Supreme Protector, the All-Knowing, the All-Wise.

5

Blessed is he that hath expended in Thy path what Thou didst bestow upon him through Thy bounty and favor. Blessed is he who, in his sore longing after Thee, hath cast away all else except Thyself. Blessed is he who hath enjoyed intimate communion with Thee, and rid himself of all attachment to any one save Thee.

6

Gird up the loins of your endeavor, O people of Bahá, that haply the tumult of religious dissension and strife that agitateth the peoples of the earth may be stilled, that every trace of it may be completely obliterated. For the love of God, and them that serve Him, arise to aid this sublime and momentous Revelation.

7

Blessed is he who hath remained faithful to My Covenant, and whom the things of the world have not kept back from attaining My Court of holiness.

8

That which thou hast heard concerning Abraham, the Friend of the All-Merciful, is the truth, and no doubt is there about it. The Voice of God commanded Him to offer up Ishmael as a sacrifice, so that His steadfastness in the Faith of God and His detachment from all else but Him may be demonstrated unto men. The purpose of God, moreover, was to sacrifice him as a ransom for the sins and iniquities of all the peoples of the earth. This same honor, Jesus, the Son of Mary, besought the one true God, exalted be His name and glory, to confer upon Him. For the same reason was Ḥusayn offered up as a sacrifice by Muḥammad, the Apostle of God.

9

In this Day, however, let them give up the life of seclusion and direct their steps towards the open world and busy themselves with that which will profit themselves and others.

10

The Great Being saith: Regard man as a mine rich in gems of inestimable value. Education can, alone, cause it to reveal its treasures, and enable mankind to benefit therefrom. If any man were to meditate on that which the Scriptures, sent down from the heaven of God's holy Will, have revealed, he would readily recognize that their purpose is that all men shall be regarded as one soul, so that the seal bearing the words "The Kingdom shall be God's" may be stamped on every heart, and the light of Divine bounty, of grace, and mercy may envelop all mankind.

11

Blessed the abased one who layeth fast hold on the cord of My glory; and the needy one who entereth beneath the shadow of the Tabernacle of My wealth. Blessed the ignorant one who seeketh the fountain of My knowledge; and the heedless one who cleaveth to the cord of My remembrance.

12

These are they who circle round the Cause of God even as the shadow doth revolve around the sun. Open, then, your eyes, O people of the Bayán, that haply ye may behold them! It is by virtue of their movement that all things are set in motion, and by reason of their stillness all things are brought to rest, would that ye might be assured thereof! Through them the believers in the Divine Unity have turned towards Him Who is the Object of the adoration of the entire creation, and by them the hearts of the righteous have found rest and composure, could ye but know it! Through them the earth hath been established, the clouds have rained down their bounty, and the bread of knowledge hath descended from the heaven of grace, could ye but perceive it!

These souls are the protectors of the Cause of God on earth, who shall preserve its beauty from the obscuring dust of idle fancies and vain imaginings. In the path of their Lord they shall not fear for their lives; rather will they sacrifice their all in their eagerness to behold the face of their Well-Beloved when once He hath appeared in this Name, the Almighty, the All-Powerful, the All-Glorious, the Most Holy.

13

Take ye counsel together, and let your concern be only for that which profiteth mankind, and bettereth the condition thereof, if ye be of them that scan heedfully.

14

O MY SERVANTS!

Ye are the trees of My garden; ye must give forth goodly and wondrous fruits, that ye yourselves and others may profit therefrom. Thus it is incumbent on every one to engage in crafts and professions, for therein lies the secret of wealth, O men of understanding! For results depend upon means, and the grace of God shall be all-sufficient unto you. Trees that yield no fruit have been and will ever be for the fire.

15

O SON OF MY HANDMAID!

Guidance hath ever been given by words, and now it is given by deeds. Every one must show forth deeds that are pure and holy, for words are the property of all alike, whereas such deeds as these belong only to Our loved ones. Strive then with heart and soul to distinguish yourselves by your deeds. In this wise We counsel you in this holy and resplendent tablet.

16

This is the Day whereon the Ocean of God's mercy hath been manifested unto men, the Day in which the Daystar of His loving-kindness hath shed its radiance upon them, the Day in which the clouds of His bountiful favor have overshadowed the whole of mankind. Now is the time to cheer and refresh the down-cast through the invigorating breeze of love and fellowship, and the living waters of friendliness and charity.

17

In like manner, every time the Prophets of God have illumined the world with the resplendent radiance of the Daystar of Divine knowledge, they have invariably summoned its peoples to embrace the light of God through such means as best befitted the exigencies of the age in which they appeared. They were thus able to scatter the darkness of ignorance, and to shed upon the world the glory of their own knowledge. It is towards the inmost essence of these Prophets, therefore, that the eye of every man of discernment must be directed, inasmuch as their one and only purpose hath always been to guide the erring, and give peace to the afflicted. . . . These are not days of prosperity and triumph. The whole of mankind is in the grip of manifold ills. Strive, therefore, to save its life through the wholesome medicine which the almighty hand of the unerring Physician hath prepared.

18

O MY SERVANT!

The best of men are they that earn a livelihood by their calling and spend upon themselves and upon their kindred for the love of God, the Lord of all worlds.

19

Glory be to Thee, O King of eternity, and the Maker of nations, and the Fashioner of every moldering bone! I pray Thee, by Thy Name through which Thou didst call all mankind unto the horizon of Thy majesty and glory, and didst guide Thy servants to the court of Thy grace and favors, to number me with such as have rid themselves from everything except Thyself, and have set themselves towards Thee, and have not been kept back by such misfortunes as were decreed by Thee, from turning in the direction of Thy gifts.

20

It beseemeth all men, in this Day, to take firm hold on the Most Great Name, and to establish the unity of all mankind. There is no place to flee to, no refuge that anyone can seek, except Him.

21

How vast is the tabernacle of the Cause of God! It hath overshadowed all the peoples and kindreds of the earth, and will, erelong, gather together the whole of mankind beneath its shelter. Thy day of service is now come. Countless Tablets bear the testimony of the bounties vouchsafed unto thee. Arise for the triumph of My Cause, and, through the power of thine utterance, subdue the hearts of men. Thou must show forth that which will ensure the peace and the well-being of the miserable and the down-trodden. Gird up the loins of thine endeavor, that perchance thou mayest release the captive from his chains, and enable him to attain unto true liberty.

22

Once more hath the eternal Spirit breathed into the mystic trumpet, and caused the dead to speed out of their sepulchers of heedlessness and error unto the realm of guidance and grace. And yet, that expectant community still crieth out: When shall these things be? When shall the promised One, the object of our expectation, be made manifest, that we may arise for the triumph of His Cause, that we may sacrifice our substance for His sake, that we may offer up our lives in His path? In like manner, have such false imaginings caused other communities to stray from the Kawthar* of

---

* *Abundance.*

the infinite mercy of Providence, and to be busied with their own idle thoughts.

23

Do not busy yourselves in your own concerns; let your thoughts be fixed upon that which will rehabilitate the fortunes of mankind and sanctify the hearts and souls of men. This can best be achieved through pure and holy deeds, through a virtuous life and a goodly behavior.

24

By the glory of Thy might, O Thou my Well-Beloved! To have sacrificed my life for the Manifestations of Thy Self, to have offered up my soul in the path of the Revealers of Thy wondrous Beauty, is to have sacrificed my spirit for Thy Spirit, my being for Thy Being, my glory for Thy glory. It is as if I had offered up all these things for Thy sake, and for the sake of Thy loved ones.

25

Put away the garment of vainglory, and divest yourselves of the attire of haughtiness. In the third of the most holy lines writ and recorded in the Ruby Tablet by the pen of the unseen this is revealed. . . .

26

Protect, moreover, O my Beloved, through Thy love for them and through the love they bear to Thee, this servant, who hath sacrificed his all for Thee, and expended whatsoever Thou hast given him in the path of Thy love and Thy good pleasure, and preserve him from all that Thou abhorrest, and from whatsoever may hinder him from entering into the Tabernacle of Thy holy sovereignty, and from attaining the seat of Thy transcendent oneness.

27

Arise, and proclaim unto the entire creation the tidings that He Who is the All-Merciful hath directed His steps towards the Ridvan and entered it. Guide, then, the people unto the garden of delight which God hath made the Throne of His Paradise. We have chosen thee to be our most mighty Trumpet, whose blast is to signalize the resurrection of all mankind.

28

I yield Thee thanks, O my God, for that Thou hast offered me up as a sacrifice in Thy path, and made me a target for the arrows of afflictions as a token of Thy love for Thy servants, and singled me out for all manner of tribulation for the regeneration of Thy people.

29

O SON OF SPIRIT!

Burst thy cage asunder, and even as the phoenix of love soar into the firmament of holiness. Renounce thyself and, filled with the spirit of mercy, abide in the realm of celestial sanctity.

30

It is incumbent upon all the peoples of the world to reconcile their differences, and, with perfect unity and peace, abide beneath the shadow of the Tree of His care and loving-kindness. It behooveth them to cleave to whatsoever will, in this Day, be conducive to the exaltation of their stations, and to the promotion of their best interests.

31

O SON OF MY HANDMAID!
    Didst thou behold immortal sovereignty, thou wouldst strive to pass from this fleeting world. But to conceal the one from thee and to reveal the other is a mystery which none but the pure in heart can comprehend.

32

Whoso followeth his Lord will renounce the world and all that is therein; how much greater, then, must be the detachment of Him Who holdeth so august a station! Forsake your palaces, and haste ye to gain admittance into His Kingdom. This, indeed, will profit you both in this world and in the next. To this testifieth the Lord of the realm on high, did ye but know it.

33

Well is it with him who, aided by the living waters of the utterance of Him Who is the Desire of all men, hath purified himself from idle fancies and vain imaginings, and torn away, in the name of the All-Possessing, the Most High, the veils of doubt, and renounced the world and all that is therein, and directed himself towards the Most Great Prison.

34

Be not dismayed, O peoples of the world, when the daystar of My beauty is set, and the heaven of My tabernacle is concealed from your eyes. Arise to further My Cause, and to exalt My Word amongst men. We are with you at all times, and shall strengthen you through the power of truth. We are truly almighty. Whoso hath recognized Me, will arise and serve Me with such determination that the powers of earth and heaven shall be unable to defeat his purpose.

35

Know thou that when the Son of Man yielded up His breath to God, the whole creation wept with a great weeping. By sacrificing Himself, however, a fresh capacity was infused into all created things. Its evidences, as witnessed in all the peoples of the earth, are now manifest before thee. The deepest wisdom which the sages have uttered, the profoundest learning which any mind hath unfolded, the arts which the ablest hands have produced, the influence exerted by the most potent of rulers, are but manifestations of the quickening power released by His transcendent, His all-pervasive, and resplendent Spirit.

36

Ye are the stars of the heaven of understanding, the breeze that stirreth at the break of day, the soft-flowing waters upon which must depend the very life of all men, the letters inscribed upon His sacred scroll. With the utmost unity, and in a spirit of perfect fellowship, exert yourselves, that ye may be enabled to achieve that which beseemeth this Day of God.

37

Blessed the insatiate soul who casteth away his selfish desires for love of Me and taketh his place at the banquet table which I have sent down from the heaven of divine bounty for My chosen ones.

38

Lay aside thy desire, and set then thine heart towards thy Lord, the Ancient of Days. We make mention of thee for the sake of God, and desire that thy name may be exalted through thy remembrance of God, the Creator of earth and heaven. . . . God hath, truly, destined a reward for thee, because of this. He, verily, will pay the doer of good his due recompense, wert thou to follow what hath been sent unto thee by Him Who is the All-Knowing, the All-Informed.

39

The true seeker hunteth naught but the object of his quest, and the lover hath no desire save union with his beloved. Nor shall the seeker reach his goal unless he sacrifice all things. That is, whatever he hath seen, and heard, and understood, all must he set at naught, that he may enter the realm of the spirit, which is the City of God.

40

Blessed the soul that hath been raised to life through My quickening breath and hath gained admittance into My heavenly Kingdom.

41

Happy are they; happy every refugee that seeketh thy shelter, in his sufferings in the path of God, the Lord of this wondrous Day! Blessed are they that remember the one true God, that magnify His Name, and seek diligently to serve His Cause. It is to these men that the sacred Books of old have referred. On them hath the Commander of the Faithful lavished his praise, saying: "The blessedness awaiting them excelleth the blessedness we now enjoy."

42

Judge fairly, I adjure thee, and arise to serve thy Lord. He, verily, shall reward thee with a reward which neither the treasures of the earth nor all the possessions of kings and rulers can equal. In all thine affairs put thy reliance in God, and commit them unto Him. He will render thee a reward which the Book hath ordained as great. Occupy thyself, during these fleeting days of thy life, with such deeds as will diffuse the fragrance of Divine good pleasure, and will be adorned with the ornament of His acceptance.

43

B lessed is the man who hath detached himself from all else but Me, hath soared in the atmosphere of My love, hath gained admittance into My Kingdom, gazed upon My realms of glory, quaffed the living waters of My bounty, hath drunk his fill from the heavenly river of My loving providence, acquainted himself with My Cause, apprehended that which I concealed within the treasury of My Words, and hath shone forth from the horizon of divine knowledge engaged in My praise and glorification. Verily, he is of Me. Upon him rest My mercy, My loving-kindness, My bounty and My glory.

FROM THE
WRITINGS OF
THE BÁB

1

The One true God may be compared unto the sun and the believer unto a mirror. No sooner is the mirror placed before the sun than it reflects its light. The unbeliever may be likened unto a stone. No matter how long it is exposed to the sunshine, it cannot reflect the sun. Thus the former layeth down his life as a sacrifice, while the latter doeth against God what he committeth. Indeed, if God willeth, He is potent to turn the stone into a mirror, but the person himself remaineth reconciled to his state. Had he wished to become a crystal, God would have made him to assume crystal form. For on that Day whatever cause prompteth the believer to believe in Him, the same will also be available to the unbeliever. But when the latter suffereth himself to be wrapt in veils, the same cause shutteth him out as by a veil.

2

Glorified art Thou, O my God! I invoke Thee by Thy Most Great Name through which the hidden secrets of God, the Most Exalted, were divulged and the kindreds of all nations converged toward the focal center of faith and certitude, through which Thy luminous Words streamed forth for the quickening of mankind and the essence of all knowledge was revealed from that Embodiment of bounty. May my life, my inmost being, my soul and my body be offered up as a sacrifice for the dust ennobled by His footsteps.

3

Let not thy tongue pay lip service in praise of God while thy heart be not attuned to the exalted Summit of Glory, and the Focal Point of communion. Thus if haply thou dost live in the Day of Resurrection, the mirror of thy heart will be set towards Him Who is the Daystar of Truth; and no sooner will His light shine forth than the splendor thereof shall forthwith be reflected in thy heart.

4

All that I beg of Thee, O my God, is to enable me, ere my soul departeth from my body, to attain Thy good-pleasure, even were it granted to me for a moment tinier than the infinitesimal fraction of a mustard seed. For if it departeth while Thou art pleased with me, then I shall be free from every concern or anxiety; but if it abandoneth me while Thou art displeased with me, then, even had I wrought every good deed, none would be of any avail, and had I earned every honor and glory, none would serve to exalt me.

5

O Lord! Assist those who have renounced all else but Thee, and grant them a mighty victory. Send down upon them, O Lord, the concourse of the angels in heaven and earth and all that is between, to aid Thy servants, to succor and strengthen them, to enable them to achieve success, to sustain them, to invest them with glory, to confer upon them honor and exaltation, to enrich them and to make them triumphant with a wondrous triumph.

6

All praise be to God Who hath, through the power of Truth, sent down this Book unto His servant, that it may serve as a shining light for all mankind. . . . Verily this is none other than the sovereign Truth; it is the Path which God hath laid out for all that are in heaven and on earth. Let him then who will, take for himself the right path unto his Lord. Verily this is the true Faith of God, and sufficient witness are God and such as are endowed with the knowledge of the Book.

FROM THE
WRITINGS AND
RECORDED
UTTERANCES OF
'ABDU'L-BAHÁ

1

Wherefore, look not on the degree of your capacity, ask not if you are worthy of the task: rest ye your hopes on the help and loving-kindness, the favors and bestowals of Bahá'u'lláh— may my soul be offered up for His friends! Urge on the steed of high endeavor over the field of sacrifice, and carry away from this wide arena the prize of divine grace.

2

As to those souls who are born into this life as ethereal and radiant entities and yet, on account of their handicaps and trials, are deprived of great and real advantages, and leave the world without having lived to the full—certainly this is a cause for grieving. This is the reason why the universal Manifestations of God unveil Their countenances to man, and endure every calamity and sore affliction, and lay down Their lives as a ransom; it is to make these very people, the ready ones, the ones who have capacity, to become dawning points of light, and to bestow upon them the life that fadeth never. This is the true sacrifice: the offering of oneself, even as did Christ, as a ransom for the life of the world.

3

For instance, consider the substance we call iron. Observe its qualities; it is solid, black, cold. These are the characteristics of iron. When the same iron absorbs heat from the fire, it sacrifices its attribute of solidity for the attribute of fluidity. It sacrifices its attribute of darkness for the attribute of light, which is a quality of the fire. It sacrifices its attribute of coldness to the quality of heat which the fire possesses so that in the iron there remains no solidity, darkness or cold. It becomes illumined and transformed, having sacrificed its qualities to the qualities and attributes of the fire.

4

Be self-sacrificing in the path of God, and wing thy flight unto the heavens of the love of the Abhá Beauty,* for any movement animated by love moveth from the periphery to the center, from space to the Daystar of the universe. Perchance thou deemest this to be difficult, but I tell thee that such cannot be the case, for when the motivating and guiding power is the divine force of magnetism it is possible, by its aid, to traverse time and space easily and swiftly.

---

* A title for Bahá'u'lláh.

5

Men keep their possessions for their own enjoyment and do not share sufficiently with others the bounty received from God. Spring is thus changed into the winter of selfishness and egotism. Jesus Christ said "Ye must be born again" so that divine Life may spring anew within you. Be kind to all around and serve one another; love to be just and true in all your dealings; pray always and so live your life that sorrow cannot touch you. Look upon the people of your own race and those of other races as members of one organism; sons of the same Father; let it be known by your behaviour that you are indeed the people of God. Then wars and disputes shall cease and over the world will spread the Most Great Peace.

6

O Lord! Make us brethren in Thy love, and cause us to be loving toward all Thy children. Confirm us in service to the world of humanity so that we may become the servants of Thy servants, that we may love all Thy creatures and become compassionate to all Thy people.

7

That is, a religious individual must disregard his personal desires and seek in whatever way he can wholeheartedly to serve the public interest; and it is impossible for a human being to turn aside from his own selfish advantages and sacrifice his own good for the good of the community except through true religious faith.

8

This evening I wish to speak to you concerning the mystery of sacrifice. There are two kinds of sacrifice: the physical and the spiritual.

9

Oye lovers of God! Do not dwell on what is coming to pass in this holy place, and be ye in no wise alarmed. Whatsoever may happen is for the best, because affliction is but the essence of bounty, and sorrow and toil are mercy unalloyed, and anguish is peace of mind, and to make a sacrifice is to receive a gift, and whatsoever may come to pass hath issued from God's grace.

10

Therefore, we learn that nearness to God is possible through devotion to Him, through entrance into the Kingdom and service to humanity; it is attained by unity with mankind and through loving-kindness to all; it is dependent upon investigation of truth, acquisition of praiseworthy virtues, service in the cause of universal peace and personal sanctification. In a word, nearness to God necessitates sacrifice of self, severance and the giving up of all to Him. Nearness is likeness.

11

Be ye confident and steadfast; your services are confirmed by the powers of heaven, for your intentions are lofty, your purposes pure and worthy. God is the helper of those souls whose aim is to serve humanity and whose efforts and endeavors are devoted to the good and betterment of all mankind.

12

O Thou divine Providence, pitiful are we, grant us Thy succor; homeless wanderers, give us Thy shelter; scattered, do Thou unite us; astray, gather us to Thy fold; bereft, do Thou bestow upon us a share and portion; athirst, lead us to the well-spring of Life; frail, strengthen us that we may arise to help Thy Cause and offer ourselves as a living sacrifice in the pathway of guidance.

13

Our greatest longing is that truth may be established in the world, and in this hope we draw near to one another in love and affection. Each and all are wholehearted and selfless, willing to sacrifice all personal ambition to the grand ideal towards which they strive: Brotherly love and peace and union among men!

14

Make peace with all the world. Love everybody; serve everybody. All are the servants of God. God has created all. He provideth for all. He is kind to all. Therefore, must we be kind to all.

15

I t is the principle that a reality sacrifices its own characteristics. Man must sever himself from the influences of the world of matter, from the world of nature and its laws; for the material world is the world of corruption and death. It is the world of evil and darkness, of animalism and ferocity, blood-thirstiness, ambition and avarice, of self-worship, egotism and passion; it is the world of nature. Man must strip himself of all these imperfections, must sacrifice these tendencies which are peculiar to the outer and material world of existence.

On the other hand, man must acquire heavenly qualities and attain divine attributes. He must become the image and likeness of God. He must seek the bounty of the eternal, become the manifestor of the love of God, the light of guidance, the tree of life and the depository of the bounties of God. That is to say, man must sacrifice the qualities and attributes of the world of nature for the qualities and attributes of the world of God.

16

I know your desire is to serve mankind, and to draw together Humanity under the banner of Oneness; but its members must beware less it become only a discussion. Look about you. How many committees have been formed, and living for a little while, have died! Committees and Societies can not create or give life.

People get together and talk, but it is God's Word alone that is powerful in its results. Consider for a moment: you would not trade together if you had no income from it and derived no benefit! Look at the followers of Christ. Their power was due to their ardour and their deeds. Every effort must have its result, else it is not a true effort. You must become the means of lighting the world of humanity. This is the infallible proof and sign. Every progress depends on two things, knowledge and practice. First acquire knowledge, and, when conviction is reached, put it into practice.

17

I n this western world with its stimulating climate, its capacities for knowledge and lofty ideals, the message of peace should be easily spread. The people are not so influenced by imitations and prejudices, and through their comprehension of the real and unreal they should attain the truth. They should become leaders in the effort to establish the oneness of humankind. What is higher than this responsibility? In the Kingdom of God no service is greater, and in the estimation of the Prophets, including Jesus Christ, there is no deed so estimable.

18

I have come to this country in the advanced years of my life, undergoing difficulties of health and climate because of excessive love for the friends of God. It is my wish that they may be assisted to become servants of the heavenly Kingdom, captives in the service of the will of God. This captivity is freedom; this sacrifice is glorification; this labor is reward; this need is bestowal. For service in love for mankind is unity with God. He who serves has already entered the Kingdom and is seated at the right hand of his Lord.

19

But we must arise in the accomplishment of its purposes, for our attention is directed toward the heavenly Kingdom unto which we must render faithful service. Therefore, all individuals present here must be in the attitude of perfect love and fellowship, manifesting the utmost humility and self-sacrifice, turning our thoughts toward the Kingdom of God so that our meeting may be an expression of the glorified hosts of the Supreme Concourse.

20

And among the teachings of Bahá'u'lláh is voluntary sharing of one's property with others among mankind. This voluntary sharing is greater than equality, and consists in this, that man should not prefer himself to others, but rather should sacrifice his life and property for others. But this should not be introduced by coercion so that it becomes a law and man is compelled to follow it. Nay, rather, man should voluntarily and of his own choice sacrifice his property and life for others, and spend willingly for the poor, just as is done in Persia among the Bahá'ís.

21

Therefore, we also must strive in this pathway of love and service, sacrificing life and possessions, passing our days in devotion, consecrating our efforts wholly to the Cause of God so that, God willing, the ensign of universal religion may be uplifted in the world of mankind and the oneness of the world of humanity be established.

22

All mankind are creatures and servants of the one God. The surface of the earth is one home; humanity is one family and household. Distinctions and boundaries are artificial, human. Why should there be discord and strife among men? All must become united and coordinated in service to the world of humanity.

23

I desire distinction for you. . . . But this distinction must not depend upon wealth—that they should become more affluent than other people. I do not desire for you financial distinction. It is not an ordinary distinction I desire; not scientific, commercial, industrial distinction. For you I desire spiritual distinction—that is, you must become eminent and distinguished in morals. In the love of God you must become distinguished from all else. You must become distinguished for loving humanity, for unity and accord, for love and justice. In brief, you must become distinguished in all the virtues of the human world—for faithfulness and sincerity, for justice and fidelity, for firmness and steadfastness, for philanthropic deeds and service to the human world, for love toward every human being, for unity and accord with all people, for removing prejudices and promoting international peace. Finally, you must become distinguished for heavenly illumination and for acquiring the bestowals of God. I desire this distinction for you. This must be the point of distinction among you.

24

Regarding the statement in The Hidden Words, that man must renounce his own self, the meaning is that he must renounce his inordinate desires, his selfish purposes and the promptings of his human self, and seek out the holy breathings of the spirit, and follow the yearnings of his higher self, and immerse himself in the sea of sacrifice, with his heart fixed upon the beauty of the All-Glorious.

25

It is now the time in the history of the world for us to strive and give an impetus to the advancement and development of inner forces—that is to say, we must arise to service in the world of morality, for human morals are in need of readjustment. We must also render service to the world of intellectuality in order that the minds of men may increase in power and become keener in perception, assisting the intellect of man to attain its supremacy so that the ideal virtues may appear.

26

The foundation of all is reality, and reality is not multiple or divisible. Moses founded it, Jesus raised its tent, and its brilliant light has shone forth in all the religions. Bahá'u'lláh proclaimed this one reality and spread the message of the Most Great Peace. Even in prison He rested not until He lighted this lamp in the East. Praise be to God! All who have accepted His teachings are lovers of peace, peacemakers ready to sacrifice their lives and expend their possessions for it. Now let this standard be upraised in the West, and many will respond to the call. America has become renowned for her discoveries, inventions and artistic skill, famous for equity of government and stupendous undertakings; now may she also become noted and celebrated as the herald and messenger of universal peace. Let this be her mission and undertaking, and may its blessed impetus spread to all countries. I pray for all of you that you may render this service to the world of humanity.

27

With reference to what is meant by an individual becoming entirely forgetful of self: the intent is that he should rise up and sacrifice himself in the true sense, that is, he should obliterate the promptings of the human condition, and rid himself of such characteristics as are worthy of blame and constitute the gloomy darkness of this life on earth—not that he should allow his physical health to deteriorate and his body to become infirm.

28

When this Cause appeared in the Orient, the friends and followers were self-sacrificing to the utmost, forfeiting everything. It is a significant and wonderful fact that, although the most precious thing on earth is life, yet twenty thousand people offered themselves willingly in the pathway of martyrdom. Recently, in Yazd two hundred of the Bahá'í friends were cruelly slain. They went to the place of martyrdom in the utmost ecstasy of attraction, smiling with joy and gratitude upon their persecutors. Some of them offered sweetmeats to their executioners, saying, "Taste of this in order that with sweetness and enjoyment you may bestow upon us the blessed cup of martyrdom."

29

This is the century of new and universal nation-hood. Sciences have advanced; industries have progressed; politics have been reformed; liberty has been proclaimed; justice is awakening. This is the century of motion, divine stimulus and accomplishment, the century of human solidarity and altruistic service, the century of universal peace and the reality of the divine Kingdom.

30

The only division that is real is this: There are heavenly men and earthly men; self-sacrificing servants of humanity in the love of the Most High, bringing harmony and unity, teaching peace and goodwill to men. On the other hand there are those selfish men, haters of their brethren, in whose hearts prejudice has replaced loving kindness, and whose influence breeds discord and strife.

31

If you plant a seed in the ground, a tree will become manifest from that seed. The seed sacrifices itself to the tree that will come from it. The seed is outwardly lost, destroyed; but the same seed which is sacrificed will be absorbed and embodied in the tree, its blossoms, fruit and branches. If the identity of that seed had not been sacrificed to the tree which became manifest from it, no branches, blossoms or fruits would have been forthcoming. . . . When you look at the tree, you will realize that the perfections, blessings, properties and beauty of the seed have become manifest in the branches, twigs, blossoms and fruit; consequently, the seed has sacrificed itself to the tree. Had it not done so, the tree would not have come into existence.

From the Writings and Recorded Utterances of 'Abdu'l-Bahá 101

32

If five people meet together to seek for truth, they must begin by cutting themselves free from all their own special conditions and renouncing all preconceived ideas. In order to find truth we must give up our prejudices, our own small trivial notions; an open receptive mind is essential. If our chalice is full of self, there is no room in it for the water of life. The fact that we imagine ourselves to be right and everybody else wrong is the greatest of all obstacles in the path towards unity, and unity is necessary if we would reach truth, for truth is one.

33

Service to humanity is service to God. Let the love and light of the Kingdom radiate through you until all who look upon you shall be illumined by its reflection. Be as stars, brilliant and sparkling in the loftiness of their heavenly station.

34

M̲an, when separated and severed from the attributes of the world of nature, sacrifices the qualities and exigencies of that mortal realm and manifests the perfections of the Kingdom, just as the qualities of the iron disappeared and the qualities of the fire appeared in their place.

35

Thus I exhort each of you, realizing its power and beauty, to sacrifice all your thoughts, words and actions to bring the knowledge of the Love of God into every heart.

36

Prophets and saints were, each and every one, subjected to the bitterest afflictions that the world has to offer, and were targets for all the cruelties and aggressions of mankind. They sacrificed their lives for the welfare of the people, and with all their hearts they hastened to the place of their martyrdom; and with their inward and outward perfections they arrayed humanity in new garments of excellent qualities, both acquired and inborn. The primary meaning of this guarding of oneself is to acquire the attributes of spiritual and material perfection.

37

In order to understand the reality of sacrifice let us consider the crucifixion and death of Jesus Christ. It is true that He sacrificed Himself for our sake. What is the meaning of this? When Christ appeared, He knew that He must proclaim Himself in opposition to all the nations and peoples of the earth. He knew that mankind would arise against Him and inflict upon Him all manner of tribulations. There is no doubt that one who put forth such a claim as Christ announced would arouse the hostility of the world and be subjected to personal abuse. He realized that His blood would be shed and His body rent by violence. Notwithstanding His knowledge of what would befall Him, He arose to proclaim His message, suffered all tribulation and hardships from the people and finally offered His life as a sacrifice in order to illumine humanity—gave His blood in order to guide the world of mankind.

38

It is appropriate and befitting that in this illumined age—the age of the progress of the world of humanity—we should be self-sacrificing and should serve the human race. Every universal cause is divine and every particular one is temporal. The principles of the divine Manifestations of God were, therefore, all-universal and all-inclusive.

39

May you all be united, may you be agreed, may you serve the solidarity of mankind. May you be well-wishers of all humanity. May you be assistants of every poor one. May you be nurses for the sick. May you be sources of comfort to the broken in heart. May you be a refuge for the wanderer. May you be a source of courage to the affrighted one. Thus, through the favor and assistance of God may the standard of the happiness of humanity be held aloft in the center of the world and the ensign of universal agreement be unfurled.

40

Until a being setteth his foot in the plane of sacrifice, he is bereft of every favor and grace; and this plane of sacrifice is the realm of dying to the self, that the radiance of the living God may then shine forth. The martyr's field is the place of detachment from self, that the anthems of eternity may be upraised. Do all ye can to become wholly weary of self, and bind yourselves to that Countenance of Splendors; and once ye have reached such heights of servitude, ye will find, gathered within your shadow, all created things. This is boundless grace; this is the highest sovereignty; this is the life that dieth not.

41

I pray that the confirmation of God may descend upon you. May you all be born again from this mortal world into the realm of the Kingdom. May you clearly witness the signs of God, sense the virtues of the divine, attain the eternal bounties and perceive the reality of everlasting life.

42

All prejudices, whether of religion, race, politics or nation, must be renounced, for these prejudices have caused the world's sickness. It is a grave malady which, unless arrested, is capable of causing the destruction of the whole human race. Every ruinous war, with its terrible bloodshed and misery, has been caused by one or other of these prejudices.

43

Souls who have hearkened to His words and accepted His message live together today in complete fellowship and love. They even offer their lives for each other. They forego and renounce worldly possessions for one another, each preferring the other to himself. This has been due to the declaration and foundation of the oneness of the world of humanity.

44

I beg of Thee by the dawning of the light of Thy Beauty that hath illumined all the earth, and by the glance of Thy divine compassion's eye that considereth all things, and by the surging sea of Thy bestowals in which all things are immersed, and by Thy streaming clouds of bounty raining down gifts upon the essences of all created things, and by the splendors of Thy mercy that existed before ever the world was—to help Thy chosen ones to be faithful, and assist Thy loved ones to serve at Thine exalted Threshold, and cause them to gain the victory through the battalions of Thy might that overpowereth all things, and reinforce them with a great fighting host from out of the Concourse on high.

45

I know it; I think a great deal of it. I know that their desire is to serve mankind. I thank this noble Society* in the name of all Bahá'ís and for myself. I hope that by God's help these friends will succeed in bringing about love and unity. It is a great work and needs the effort of all the servants of God!

---

* Theosophical Society. 'Abdu'l-Bahá was addressing a group of Theosophists in London.

46

Christ declared, "Many are called but few are chosen." Verily, God has chosen you for His love and knowledge; God has chosen you for the worthy service of unifying mankind; God has chosen you for the purpose of investigating reality and promulgating international peace; God has chosen you for the progress and development of humanity, for spreading and proclaiming true education, for the expression of love toward your fellow creatures and the removal of prejudice; God has chosen you to blend together human hearts and give light to the human world. The doors of His generosity are wide, wide open to us; but we must be attentive, alert and mindful, occupied with service to all mankind, appreciating the bestowals of God and ever conforming to His will.

47

O Thou merciful God! O Thou Who art mighty and powerful! O Thou most kind Father! These servants have gathered together, turning to Thee, supplicating Thy threshold, desiring Thine endless bounties from Thy great assurance. They have no purpose save Thy good pleasure. They have no intention save service to the world of humanity.

O God! Make this assemblage radiant. Make the hearts merciful. Confer the bounties of the Holy Spirit. Endow them with a power from heaven. Bless them with heavenly minds. Increase their sincerity, so that with all humility and contrition they may turn to Thy kingdom and be occupied with service to the world of humanity. May each one become a radiant candle. May each one become a brilliant star. May each one become beautiful in color and redolent of fragrance in the Kingdom of God.

48

There are no solitaries and no hermits among the Bahá'ís. Man must work with his fellows. Everyone should have some trade, or art or profession, be he rich or poor, and with this he must serve humanity. This service is acceptable as the highest form of worship.

49

Consider: We plant a seed. A complete and perfect tree appears from it, and from each seed of this tree another tree can be produced. Therefore, the part is expressive of the whole, for this seed was a part of the tree, but therein potentially was the whole tree. So each one of us may become expressive or representative of all the bounties of life to mankind. This is the unity of the world of humanity. This is the bestowal of God. This is the felicity of the human world, and this is the manifestation of the divine favor.

NOTES

From the Writings of Bahá'u'lláh

1. *Tablets of Bahá'u'lláh,* p. 263.
2. *Gleanings from the Writings of Bahá'u'lláh,* no. 28.1.
3. *Tablets of Bahá'u'lláh,* p. 17.
4. *Gleanings from the Writings of Bahá'u'lláh,* no. 68.7.
5. *Prayers and Meditations,* p. 33.
6. Epistle to the Son of the Wolf, pp. 13–14.
7. *Tablets of Bahá'u'lláh,* p. 17.
8. *Gleanings from the Writings of Bahá'u'lláh,* no. 32.1.
9. *Tablets of Bahá'u'lláh,* p. 24.
10. *Gleanings from the Writings of Bahá'u'lláh,* no. 122.1.
11. *Tablets of Bahá'u'lláh,* p. 16.
12. *The Summons of the Lord of Hosts,* nos. 1.15–16.

13. *Gleanings from the Writings of Bahá'u'lláh,* no. 120.1.

14. The Hidden Words, Persian, no. 80.

15. Ibid., no. 76.

16. *Gleanings from the Writings of Bahá'u'lláh,* no. 5.1.

17. Ibid., no. 34.6.

18. The Hidden Words, Persian, no. 82.

19. *Prayers and Meditations,* p. 47–48.

20. *Gleanings from the Writings of Bahá'u'lláh,* no. 100.7.

21. Ibid., no. 43.1.

22. The Kitáb-i-Íqán, ¶25.

23. *Gleanings from the Writings of Bahá'u'lláh,* no. 43.4.

24. *Prayers and Meditations by Bahá'u'lláh,* pp. 95–96.

25. The Hidden Words, Persian no. 47.

26. *Prayers and Meditations,* p. 337.

27. *Gleanings from the Writings of Bahá'u'lláh,* no. 14.10.

28. *Prayers and Meditations,* p. 154.

29. The Hidden Words, Persian, no. 38.

30. *Gleanings from the Writings of Bahá'u'lláh,* no. 4.1.

31. The Hidden Words, Persian, no. 41.

32. The Kitáb-i-Aqdas, ¶83.

33. Epistle to the Son of the Wolf, p. 42.

34. *Gleanings from the Writings of Bahá'u'lláh*, no. 71.1.

35. Ibid., no. 36.1.

36. Ibid., no. 96.3.

37. *Tablets of Bahá'u'lláh*, p. 16.

38. *The Summons of the Lord of Hosts*, no. 1.172.

39. The Seven Valleys, p. 7.

40. *Tablets of Bahá'u'lláh*, p. 16.

41. *Gleanings from the Writings of Bahá'u'lláh*, no. 55.3.

42. Epistle to the Son of the Wolf, p. 76.

43. *Tablets of Bahá'u'lláh*, p. 16.

From the Writings of the Báb

1. *Selections from the Writings of the Báb*, no. 3:31:1.

2. Ibid., no. 7:29:4.

3. Ibid., no. 3:21:1.

4. Ibid., no. 7:18:3.

5. Ibid., no. 7:23:2.

6. Ibid., no. 2:1:1.

From the Writings and Recorded Utterances of 'Abdu'l-Bahá

1. *Selections from the Writings of 'Abdu'l-Bahá,* no. 8.5.
2. Ibid., no. 31.8.
3. *The Promulgation of Universal Peace,* pp. 636–37.
4. *Selections from the Writings of 'Abdu'l-Bahá,* no. 166.1.
5. *'Abdu'l-Bahá in London,* pp. 82–83.
6. *The Promulgation of Universal Peace,* pp. 419–20.
7. *The Secret of Divine Civilization,* ¶170.
8. *The Promulgation of Universal Peace,* p. 632.
9. *Selections from the Writings of 'Abdu'l-Bahá,* no. 200.10.
10. *The Promulgation of Universal Peace,* pp. 204–5.
11. Ibid., p. 632.
12. *Selections from the Writings of 'Abdu'l-Bahá,* no. 233.17.
13. *Paris Talks,* no. 32.4.
14. *The Promulgation of Universal Peace,* p. 492.
15. Ibid., p. 636.
16. *'Abdu'l-Bahá in London,* p. 108.

17. *The Promulgation of Universal Peace,* p. 115.

18. Ibid., p. 259.

19. Ibid., p. 473.

20. *Selections from the Writings of 'Abdu'l-Bahá,* no. 227.19.

21. *The Promulgation of Universal Peace,* p. 202.

22. Ibid., p. 149.

23. Ibid., pp. 265–66.

24. *Selections from the Writings of 'Abdu'l-Bahá,* no. 181.1.

25. *The Promulgation of Universal Peace,* p. 462.

26. Ibid., p. 169.

27. *Selections from the Writings of 'Abdu'l-Bahá,* no. 153.6.

28. *The Promulgation of Universal Peace,* pp. 541–42.

29. Ibid., p. 195.

30. *Paris Talks,* no. 45.14.

31. *The Promulgation of Universal Peace,* pp. 635–36.

32. *Paris Talks,* no. 41.7.

33. *The Promulgation of Universal Peace,* p. 10.

34. Ibid., p. 637.

35. *Paris Talks,* no. 27.11.

36. *The Secret of Divine Civilization,* ¶63.

37. *The Promulgation of Universal Peace,* p. 634.

38. *Selections from the Writings of 'Abdu'l-Bahá,* no. 34.1.

39. *The Promulgation of Universal Peace,* p. 599.

40. *Selections from the Writings of 'Abdu'l-Bahá,* no. 36.5.

41. *The Promulgation of Universal Peace,,* p. 472.

42. *Paris Talks,* no. 45.1.

43. *The Promulgation of Universal Peace,* p. 556.

44. *Selections from the Writings of 'Abdu'l-Bahá,* no. 2.6.

45. *'Abdu'l-Bahá in London,* p. 61.

46. *The Promulgation of Universal Peace,* p. 474.

47. Ibid., pp. 75–76.

48. *'Abdu'l-Bahá in London,* p. 93.

49. *The Promulgation of Universal Peace,* p. 21.

BIBLIOGRAPHY

Works of Bahá'u'lláh

Epistle to the Son of the Wolf. New ed. Translated by Shoghi Effendi. 1st ps ed. Wilmette, IL: Bahá'í Publishing Trust, 1988.

Gleanings from the Writings of Bahá'u'lláh. Translated by Shoghi Effendi. Wilmette, IL: Bahá'í Publishing, 2005.

The Hidden Words. Translated by Shoghi Effendi. Wilmette, IL: Bahá'í Publishing, 2002.

The Kitáb-i-Aqdas: The Most Holy Book. 1st ps ed. Wilmette, IL: Bahá'í Publishing Trust, 1993.

The Kitáb-i-Íqán: The Book of Certitude. Translated by Shoghi Effendi. Wilmette, IL: Bahá'í Publishing, 2003.

The Pen of Glory: Selected Works of Bahá'u'lláh. Wilmette, IL: Bahá'í Publishing, 2008.

Prayers and Meditations. Translated by Shoghi Effendi. 1st pocket-size ed. Wilmette, IL: Bahá'í Publishing Trust, 1987.

The Seven Valleys and the Four Valleys. New ed. Translated by Ali-Kuli Khan and Marzieh Gail. Wilmette, IL: Bahá'í Publishing Trust, 1991.

The Summons of the Lord of Hosts: Tablets of Bahá'u'lláh. Wilmette, IL: Bahá'í Publishing, 2006.

Tablets of Bahá'u'lláh revealed after the Kitáb-i-Aqdas. Compiled by the Research Department of the Universal House of Justice. Translated by Habib Taherzadeh et al. Wilmette, IL: Bahá'í Publishing Trust, 1988.

Works of the Báb

Selections from the Writings of the Báb. Compiled by the Research Department of the Universal House of Justice. Translated by Habib Taherzadeh et al. Wilmette, IL: Bahá'í Publishing Trust, 2006.

Works of 'Abdu'l-Bahá

'Abdu'l-Bahá in London: Addresses &Notes of Conversations. London: Bahá'í Publishing Trust, 1987.

Paris Talks: Addresses Given By 'Abdu'l-Bahá in Paris in 1911. Wilmette, IL: Bahá'í Publishing, 2011.

Promulgation of Universal Peace: Talks Delivered by 'Abdu'l-Bahá during His Visit to the United States and Canada in 1912. Compiled by Howard MacNutt. Wilmette, IL: Bahá'í Publishing, 2012.

The Secret of Divine Civilization. Translated by Marzieh Gail and Ali-Kuli Khan. Wilmette, IL: Bahá'í Publishing, 2007.

Selections from the Writings of 'Abdu'l-Bahá. Compiled by the Research Department of the Universal House of Justice. Translated by a Committee at the Bahá'í World Center and Marzieh Gail. Wilmette, IL: Bahá'í Publishing, 2010.

Some Answered Questions. Compiled and translated by Laura Clifford Barney. 1st pocket-size ed. Wilmette, IL: Bahá'í Publishing Trust, 1984.

Bahá'í Compilations

*Bahá'í Prayers: A Selection of Prayers Revealed by Bahá'u'lláh,
the Báb, and 'Abdu'l-Bahá*. Wilmette, IL: Bahá'í
Publishing Trust, 2008.

PUBLISHING

Bahá'í Publishing and the Bahá'í Faith

Bahá'í Publishing produces books based on the teachings of the Bahá'í Faith. Founded over 160 years ago, the Bahá'í Faith has spread to some 235 nations and territories and is now accepted by more than five million people. The word "Bahá'í" means "follower of Bahá'u'lláh." Bahá'u'lláh, the founder of the Bahá'í Faith, asserted that He is the Messenger of God for all of humanity in this day. The cornerstone of His teachings is the establishment of the spiritual unity of humankind, which will be achieved by personal transformation and the application of clearly identified spiritual principles. Bahá'ís also believe that there is but one religion and that all the Messengers of God—among them Abraham, Zoroaster, Moses, Krishna, Buddha, Jesus, and Muḥammad—have progressively revealed its nature. Together, the world's great religions are expressions of a single, unfolding divine plan. Human beings, not God's Messengers, are the source of religious divisions, prejudices, and hatreds.

The Bahá'í Faith is not a sect or denomination of another religion, nor is it a cult or a social movement. Rather, it is a globally recognized independent world religion founded on new books of scripture revealed by Bahá'u'lláh.

Bahá'í Publishing is an imprint of the National Spiritual Assembly of the Bahá'ís of the United States.

For more information about the Bahá'í Faith,
or to contact Bahá'ís near you,
visit http://www.bahai.us/
or call
1-800-22-UNITE

Other Books Available from Bahá'í Publishing

AWAKENING
A HISTORY OF THE BÁBÍ AND BAHÁ'Í FAITHS IN NAYRÍZ
Hussein Ahdieh and Hillary Chapman
$17.00 US / $19.00 CAN
Trade Paper
ISBN 978-1-61851-029-7

An eye-opening account of brutal religious persecution and a discussion of the dangers of fanaticism and the importance of religious tolerance.

Awakening: A History of the Bábí and Bahá'í Faiths in Nayríz is an inspiring account of the brutal religious persecutions that took place in 1850, 1853, and 1909 in the town of Nayríz, Iran, against its Bábí and Bahá'í residents. During this time, the town's citizens, spurred on by a corrupt Muslim clergy and government, launched several waves of bloodshed against the Bábís—and later Bahá'ís—who lived there. This type of persecution continues today in present-day Iran toward the Bahá'ís—on a more subtle level—and the history of the Bábís and Bahá'ís in Nayríz serves as a reminder of what can happen when religious fanaticism and paranoia are allowed to replace rational thinking and tolerance.

CALL TO REMEMBRANCE
THE LIFE OF BAHÁ'U'LLÁH IN HIS OWN WORDS
Geoffrey Marks
$17.00 US / $19.00 CAN
Trade Paper
ISBN 978-1-61851-030-3

An excellent introduction to the distinction and purity of the life of Bahá'u'lláh, the Prophet-Founder of the Bahá'í Faith.

Call to Remembrance is the first book to tell the story of Bahá'u'lláh, the Prophet-Founder of the Bahá'í Faith, largely through His own words. Combining extracts from Bahá'u'lláh's writing and supplementing with additional background information, many major events in His life and ministry are presented. This unique compilation chronicles all periods of Bahá'u'lláh's life, and is organized into five sections.

PRAYERS FOR CHILDREN
Constanze von Kitzing
$12.00 US / $14.00 CAN
Paper Over Board
ISBN 978-1-61851-032-7

A beautifully illustrated collection of Bahá'í prayers for children; a perfect book for the whole family to treasure.

Prayers for Children is a collection of Bahá'í prayers compiled specifically for young children. Beautifully illustrated, this book will help parents cultivate a lifelong habit of daily prayer in their child. The beautiful color illustrations will appeal to children of all ages and will make it an appealing book for daily use for parents and children alike.